DO MORE WITH LESS

Lead A Meaningful Life Through Daily Practice To Declutter Your Mind And Reach True Happiness

DR. CHLOE WHITE

ISBN: 9781657839922

TEXT COPYRIGHT © [DR. CHLOE WHITE]

Opening words

It's not just you! Many others can't seem to reach what they set out to achieve due to a lack of resources such as time, money, and energy. The simple answer would be to make more of those resources. But how?

Everyone has the same twenty-four-hour day – no more, no less. We all have finite energy and strength. So, how do some people work more efficiently and achieve more success? The reason is that they know how to prioritize the things that matter and let go of those that don't. That is essentially what "declutter" means. With less stuff and an organized living environment, your life will be happier and meaningful.

This eBook will give you a map to guide your steps as you start the journey towards a meaningful life. It will help you see what is essential and what is not and how you can dispose of the latter. It covers fundamental areas in your life, starting with a small corner in your home, your digital space, and your daily activities. When you start applying the simple practices in this book, you will see significant changes in the way you live and how you appreciate life.

I hope this book brings you ever closer to reaching a happier life. I also hope you have a delightful time reading this book.

CHAPTER I: WHY YOU NEED TO DECLUTTER YOUR LIFE

1. One way to declutter: Minimalism

When you hear the word "Minimalism," what is the first image that pops into your mind? Is it the boy you read about on the news, who sold his house and all his belongings to live a life on the road? Or is it an Instagram post from a person bragging about how they have only two shirts, two pants, and a bed at home? Perhaps, it is the image of that famous person who owns fifty-two things and travels all over the world?

Trust me; you don't need to go to those extremes to improve your life.

So, let's first find out what exactly is Minimalism and why is there so much hype around it. In the most basic sense, Minimalism means living with only the essential items. These are the things you need and the items that truly matter in your life; the rest is discarded. Your material possessions do not define your life. However, with ubiquitous advertisements and feverish capitalism, we sometimes forget about that fact. So we keep filling our houses and our every moment with unnecessary things, hoping that they will somehow give us fulfillment. Minimalism allows you to take a good honest look at your home and your life, and it helps you decide what changes are needed.

A minimalist mindset is about letting go and making permanent life changes.

I'm sure you're wondering: "Really? How could my life be better with less?" It'll take some time and effort, but I'm sure that in the end, you will find it a refreshing change.

Let me guide you in the first few stages - the essential steps to a whole new journey of Minimalism.

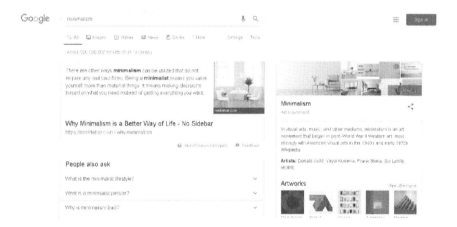

Search for "Minimalism" on Google will get you over 326 billion search results!

2. Why should I declutter my life?

People decide to declutter their lives for various reasons. However, when they see that it has no benefits or any real impact on their life, they probably won't maintain the lifestyle for long. On the contrary, here are some of the actual changes that you'll definitely see when you start simplifying your life:

- *Space for what matters* - You will have more time and more money to pursue what is most significant to you. You'll need less time to tidy up your wardrobe or clean up your home. It goes without saying that this practice will help eliminate much of the unnecessary stresses in life while also welcoming more positive thoughts.

- *A clear mind*: When there is more clean space in your home and surroundings, you will have more clarity of mind and thought. A calmer and less agitated mind will also mean more creative ideas and more nurturing, better relationships

- *Freedom*: A famous saying laments, "*We buy things we don't need with money we don't have to impress people we don't like.*" When we break away from the habit of purchasing and filling our houses with things only to impress, we'll be able to redefine the meaning of success and stop living for other people. The way we think about personal values will change. Thus, your mind will be free to think about fulfilling your purpose, instead of seeking an escape by adding items to your cart.

- *Positive lifestyle and mindset changes*: Greed is one of the primary reasons for the unhappiness that people feel today. If you pursue material things, experiences, and relationships only for that next Instagram-worthy photo, you will never find satisfaction in life. On the other hand, minimalism promotes a lifestyle that helps you slow down, ignore the outside noise, and focus on what truly matters.

- *Eco-conscious habits*: When you consume and waste less, you are contributing towards a greener and less polluted planet. Consumerism accounts for up to 60 percent of global greenhouse gas emissions. Just think about all the packages and plastic wrapping that comes from buying all those products.

Now, you're ready to take the first steps in this new and exciting journey to improving your lifestyle.

CHAPTER II: ESSENTIAL PRACTICES

1. Fundamental rules

Know your WHY

People are motivated to make life changes for different reasons. Perhaps, they read something life-changing in a blog post, in the advice of a friend, or just like you, in the words of an eBook. No matter how they arrive at this point, they all do it for the same reason: They want to be happier, and they want to attain a meaningful life. But that reason is not good enough!

You want your motivation to make the needed changes to be specific. It's not easy to suddenly start making changes to the lifestyle to which you've become accustomed. If you don't have a particular motivation, you won't be able to sustain your determination to keep going and not give up.

Therefore, make sure that you know your intentions and motivations before you start. Is it because you want a clearer mind and less stress in life? Perhaps you want to contribute to movements that care for the environment? Or, you want to save time and money and be able to focus on what matters in your life? Think about these points carefully before you start this journey.

Declutter before organizing

I know that you're eager to make changes in your house, daily routine, and, ultimately, your life. However, you can't start shuffling things around before making space for them. The core concept of minimalism is to reduce the number of items that you have in your life. Therefore, you need to declutter before anything else.

Prioritize

In this journey, you'll need to make a lot of choices. There'll be some decisions that you'll find hard to make. Although you're always encouraged to go with your instincts and avoid overanalyzing things, you might still get confused at times. Priorities exist to rescue you!

You could start establishing priorities by thinking about your daily needs, personal values, and current projects. For example:

- If you're trying to get fit, you might decide to keep your gym clothes and gear just yet
- If you're a book-lover and enjoy the smell of a paper book, you don't have to get rid of your entire collection

You could begin asking yourself questions like:" *What are the things that make you happy" "What is a part of you that you can't live without?"*

You will get a more definite sense of your priorities when you start decluttering. Hence, all you have to do now is start thinking about it.

-Simple home decor-

<u>Decide what's right for you</u>

This is not a competition! People with the fewest items in their homes won't be crowned as winners while everyone else loses. Nothing can be farther from the truth.

There is no set number of clothes, shoes, or chairs that you should own. It all depends on you and where you currently are in life. Do everything at your own pace, as you see fit, and prioritize what will suit you best at this moment.

2. Start with your wardrobe

It's not surprising that clothes are one of the items that you're most likely to over-buy. You might even have so much that you tend to forget which clothes you might already have. So, you end up buying more because you think you've nothing new to wear. Interestingly, your wardrobe will show the most apparent changes when you start applying the principles here.

-Once you have decluttered your clothes, you will start to believe in the power of minimalism -

First, I will present some fantastic benefits of a minimalist wardrobe:

- Fewer clothes mean less time spent choosing the "right" outfit when going out. You won't have to spend hours in from of the mirror wondering: "Do I look good in this shirt/ pants?"
- Fewer clothes also mean a shorter time spent doing the laundry, ironing, and organizing your wardrobe.

Before decluttering, you need to do some self-examination and answer the following questions:

- What kind of weather and climate is normal where I live?

- What are my daily activities, and which places do I often visit? Trust me; you don't want to be stuck with only 1 or 2 outfit options for both the office and the gym especially in seasonal climates.

Now, let's work on the definition of your "wardrobe." It means:

- Clothes

- Jewelry and accessories

- Shoes

- Bags

-A girl's wardrobe could possibly look like this -

Here are the steps towards a minimalist closet:

Step 1: Look

Take your entire wardrobe – all of your clothes, jewelry, accessories, bags, and shoes – and put them in one place where you can see them. Remember, you need to be able to see ALL of them together.

I'm sure memories will flood your mind as you look at each piece: the ones you bought for special occasions, the ones gifted to you by a loved one, and even the ones you've forgotten you had.

Take a close look because it's about to get real!

Step 2: Categorize

First, make sure that your floor is clean. Afterward, move all your stuff on the floor. You'll need the space to accomplish this step.

You'll be assorting your items in four piles:

- Love: Things that still make your heart flutter when you see them and are inseparable from you. You need them, and you feel like you'll love them forever.
- Maybe: It feels, somehow, unnecessary to keep them, but you can't seem to let them go.
- Giveaway: You don't see yourself using them in the future, but they're still in good condition
- Trash: They look old or terrible, so much so that you'll feel embarrassed giving them away

Try not to overthink. Instead, go with your intuition and gut.

Remember to keep going until you finish sorting your entire wardrobe. You can, of course, take a break, eat a snack, or chat with a friend. Just don't give up until you're done!

When you finish categorizing all the items, pat yourself on the back and whisper: "Good job!" We're almost there. Now, only two piles need your attention: Love and Maybe. You can do this next exercise on your own, or you could ask a trusted friend to help.

Now, try on different outfits with the accessories and shoes. Afterward, look at yourself in the mirror and ask both yourself and for your friend's thoughts:

"Would I go to the store and buy this outfit today?"

Do I see myself wearing it in the next 3 to 6 months?

If any of the answers are no, you can confidently include it with the Giveaway pile without looking back. After a while, you might even forget you had it.

Step 3: Organize

It's now time to return the clothes that you love so dearly back into your closet. We stand by the KonMari method of folding clothes and store them upright so that you could clearly see each item you own. This method accomplishes two things: it contributes to a more organized life, and it keeps you from buying unnecessary things in the future.

- *Choosing clothes in similar and complementing colors will make it easy for you to mix and match -*

Extra notes:

1. Make sure to keep pieces of clothes that are easy to mix and match. To do that, you should check the extent of the color palette and style of your new wardrobe.

2. Don't be too upset if you couldn't get rid of too many clothes at first. Minimalism is the journey of change, and people can take it at their own pace

3. **Example of a minimalist closet:**

Remember that this example is only a guide and not a specific checklist.

- **Jeans**: One to three pairs in black, light, or dark blue.

- **Dark leggings:** 1-3 pairs
- **Nightwear pants:** 1-3 pairs
- **Shorts:**
    - 1-3 pairs of **jean shorts** in black, blue, or white.
    - 1-2 pairs of **sports shorts** for running and the gym.
- **Bras:** 6-7 bras. Two in dark and nude for daily use — your choice of bralette and strapless, preferably in black and white.
    - **Sports bras:** Two that are either high impact or low impact.
- **Tops:** 15 tops with different functions (tanks, t-shirts, long-sleeves, gym clothes, etc.).
- **Bulky sweaters:** 2-3 bulky sweaters.
- **Dresses:** 4 dresses of your choice.
- **Skirts:** 2 - 3 skirts; Include both long and short.
- **Jackets:** 4 jackets:
    - Brown leather jacket
    - Lightweight easy-to-pack coat
    - Ski jacket
    - Winter coat
- **Bags:** 2 bags
    - A backpack is big enough for school or weekend trips.
    - A small body bag for quick trips when you don't need to carry much.

- **Accessories:** 2 hats, 2 scarves, and 1-2 earrings
- **Shoes:** 2-3 pairs of sports shoes, sandals, and heels.

3. Your house

The next step will now be on a bigger scale! Since you've got your wardrobe under control, we will move on to your home. When you've reached this final stage's finish line, you will have a sense of power and accomplishment whenever you walk into your lovely and decluttered house.

Our strategy we'll be to go room by room. We'll look into each of your home's rooms and tackle them bit by bit.

- A home can take various shapes and sizes -

Here are some tips before you start:

- You need to look at every nook and cranny carefully. Pay attention to the places you might usually ignore such as under your mattress, your walls, your bedroom floor, and many other areas you don't often see.
- Declutter one room at a time. You might be really eager to tidy up your space but don't start cleaning up your living room when you're still organizing your kitchen, Finish what you're doing in one room first, then move on to the next.

Be patient! I don't know how many rooms you have, but this process will likely take more time than your wardrobe. It'll be worth it, though. If necessary, you can create a schedule that indicates a deadline for each room to ensure you won't procrastinate before getting the job done.

This entire process will be fundamentally similar to what you have done with your closet, just with some additional steps.

Step 1: LOOK

Gather all the items in your chosen room to a place where they can be clearly seen. It could on the floor or a large table. Don't forget to search in the hidden spaces for surprising things that may have disappeared from your memory.

Step 2: CATEGORIZE

Sort the items into the same four categorize as you did with your wardrobe.

- Love: Things you can't live without and will surely use more of in the future.
- Maybe: They feel too precious to give away, but you don't see yourself getting much value from them.
- Giveaway: Somebody will be happy to receive these once-loved items now that you don't need them anymore.
- Trash: They are unusable and should be discarded.

Again, don't put too much thought into the categories. Follow your instincts.

Step 3: ORGANIZE

Take one more look at every item in the Love and Maybe groups. Ask yourself the following questions:

- Are you going to use them in 3 to 6 months?
- Do they make you happy when you hold them?

Step 4: STORE

Unlike your wardrobe, tidying up your home requires an extra step: Store. This activity is a crucial step in transforming your home's appearance. If you do this step well, you won't have to declutter your home again any time soon. It revolves around the idea of organizing the right things in the right place.

Here are a few fundamental rules for efficient storing:

- Before organizing, make sure to clean your drawers, boxes, containers, cabinets, and shelves. A great time to do this is when you've gathered all the items in a room in one spot.

- Determine which items will be in constant use and which things can go to storage. For example, you likely wouldn't store the items that you use on a daily basis, such as your plates, bowls, cups, and cutlery. Meanwhile, you may want to put things like souvenirs, pictures, book collections, or shoes in a specific area in your house to keep them in good condition. You'll also know precisely where they are when you need them. On the other hand, you should put away the items you currently don't need, such as seasonal clothes or notebooks for next semester.

- Store similar items together. Of course, you'll want to keep all your kitchen tools and clothes as well as other things like gardening tools and photography equipment in one place. It will take less time and energy to find them. Meanwhile, you could use dividers or small containers to store all the smaller items like accessories (earrings, necklaces, etc.), stationery (pens, highlighters, post-it notes, etc.), make-up, and skincare items.

- To maximize your storage space, you should consider using suitable storage items such as shelves in the living room, drawers in the bedroom, and cabinets in the bathroom. You should also make the most of unused spaces such as the areas above your kitchen cabinets. You could add more hangers in your closet, use doors to hang clothes or pictures or use storage options specifically designed to save or maximize space.

These notes will be invaluable as you declutter one room after another, making this journey much easier.

Bathroom

Be mindful of expiration dates. Using products past their expiry date can be harmful. Any products past this date or those you haven't used for a long time deserve to go.

If you use a cabinet or drawers, you should put the items that you use most often on the top drawers.

Meanwhile, keep similar items together. For example, place products used for your hair in one place and likewise for body care and skincare products. If you find unused small boxes or plastic containers as you declutter your rooms, make sure to put them to good use here.

A tidy bathroom is also a safe bathroom where accidents are less likely to happen

Bedroom

The first thing you should do, without exception, is to make your bed. It will help both clear your mind and create that initial sense of tidiness in your room.

The hidden spaces in your bedroom may include your clothes stand, above cabinets, under your bed, and beside your windows.

You'll want to check every corner, so you're sure you didn't miss any spots.

Kitchen

Organizing your kitchen should be at the very top of your priority list. Like your bathroom, you should categorize and gather similar items into groups and find a specific place for them. These items could be your baking tools, cutting boards, glassware, and utensils.

Since the kitchen is almost always the busiest part of the house, make sure to clean and organize it daily.

- An organized kitchen will motivate you to cook more -

Living room

Decide on a permanent space for the commonly used items in your living room, like remote controls, magazines, and books.

Study the entire space of your living room then ask yourself these questions:

"Am I decorating too much?" and,

"Which décor could I put away to make this living room look better?"

After you've successfully decluttered your home, remember to relax, acknowledge the effort you've done, and commend yourself. Do this no matter the number of items you were able to discard. Breathe in deep, and exhale slowly. Afterward, consider the checklist below and try to figure out where you can improve to make your house even more beautiful:

Clear surfaces: In your minimalist home, all the surfaces should be clear of all items, except for one or two. There should be no stacks of books, papers, or any other objects randomly lying on any tables.

Blank walls: Except for a few memorable pictures and meaningful artworks, your walls should be bare.

Clear floors: To be cluttered, stacked on, or used for storage is not your floor's purpose. The only stuff that should be on it is your furniture.

If you store stuff out of sight as recommended above, you should know precisely what you're storing and what they mean to you and your life. If not, you should consider donating or discarding them.

Although the décor you end up choosing is entirely up to you, try to keep it as simple as possible.

Now, look at your new home. How do you feel about it? I hope you're feeling proud and relieved.

4. Your daily routine

Food

When one is living a busy lifestyle in a big city away from parents or relatives, one of the questions that may bother them every day is, "What should I eat today?". As we all know, eating out is expensive and could be unhealthy. On the other hand, cooking for yourself could be frustrating or merely a burden. By keeping your eating habits simple, according to your minimalist lifestyle, you can save so much time, money, and energy. Even more importantly, It can contribute to more happiness in your life.

Here is a simple approach to your diet:

Staple meals:

You should plan for staple meals that you can cook again and again. These meals should be healthful, wholesome, and provide adequate nutrition. Ideally, they should suit your tastes while also easy to make. Thus, you can come back to them regularly without getting bored or sick of them.

Nutritional meal:

You can't sustain this lifestyle, or any lifestyle for that matter if you don't maintain a healthy body. According to the ***Canada Food***

Guide 2018:

- 50% of your diet should be vegetables and fruits
- 25% should be whole grain food like bread, mixed rice, or noodles
- The remaining 25% should be healthy protein sources such as eggs, beans, nuts, and meats.

Although you can decide on your drink of choice, the best option is still plain water.

To maximize the quality of your meal, you should also:

- Be mindful of your eating habits. For example, do you often do other activities like reading, watching TV, etc. while eating? Do you quickly swallow food after chewing only a few times?
- Eat with people more.
- Read food nutrition labels.
- Limit foods high in sodium, sugar, or saturated fat.
- Be aware of food marketing.

Meal prep

You can do your groceries on the weekends and prepare food for a whole week or half of the week. It will save you time while keeping regularly cooking at home from becoming a tiresome chore.

Try to make breakfast for the entire week. For example, you can make enough salad for several portions that can last you the entire day, or you can make a big batch of your favorite dish, so you'll always have dinners ready ahead of time. You'll only need to reheat them.

It'll take time for you to get used to meal prepping. There will be hits and misses, and you may have to experiment a lot. Be patient and be open to trying new things. Eventually, you'll find a system and meal combinations that will suit your tastes and lifestyle.

Minimalist-style kitchen

Keeping a minimalist kitchen will help you cut all that time spent deciding which food to eat and sorting all the varieties. It will also dramatically reduce your food waste.

Again, how you adjust your kitchen will depend on your preference. Here are some helpful suggestions:

Dry food

- Nuts & Seeds
- Grains: oats and your favorite type of rice
- Other grains: quinoa, barley, couscous, bulgur, and the like
- Varieties of pasta and noodles

Canned foods

- Tomatoes
- Tomato sauce

- Fruit
- Coconut milk

Beans & Lentils

Dried fruit

Other dried goods

- Cereal
- Peanut butter
- Favorite crackers
- Dark chocolate
- Cornstarch

Baking supplies

- Flour
- Sugar
- Baking powder
- Cocoa powder
- Chocolate chips
- Vanilla extract

Oils and vinegar

Herbs and spices

Conversely, Here are items you should avoid in your minimalist kitchen:

- Chips
- Soda
- Candy
- Heat-and-eat meals
- Canned/instant soup

-A good life starts with good food -

To make things easier, here are some tips that you can learn by heart:

- Buy only what you need. Avoid restocking your fridge or pantry before you've consumed the items you've brought home from your last grocery trip.
- Aim to cook at home as much as possible and avoid eating out.

- Make sure to organize your pantry. Clear out and clean the counters after every kitchen session.

- You don't need fancy, single-use kitchen tools. Keep them simple.

- Reduce food waste as much as possible.

- Store only basic ingredients or those you use regularly. Filling your fridge and cupboards with every kind of sauce, seasoning, pasta shape, etc. is not necessary.

- Choose simple, whole, and minimally-processed foods.

- Be flexible. Learn to be adaptable as you change and modify your diet depending on your taste and health needs.

Your bag, purse, and packing habits

What you carry with you every day can make a massive difference in your life. Simplifying your everyday carry can reduce stress and save time. You'd be entering the world with a lighter heart. What may be the most challenging part of this exercise is determining what is essential and how much is enough. Here are some important notes to help you answer that question:

- **Identify your needs.** Naturally, a 20-year-old female student's purse will look utterly different from the bag of a middle-aged working man. Having a good understanding of both your habits and lifestyle will help you make wise decisions. For example, you don't need to force yourself to get rid of your scented candles especially when it helps you sleep. Remember, sacrificing conveniences too soon will make it challenging to keep this fabulous lifestyle for the long-term.

- **Review after each trip.** As mentioned above, organizing your everyday carry won't be a walk in the park. So, take your time. Initially, you might pack too much or too little. However, with practice and careful consideration after each try, your packing skills will get better over time.

- **Consider travel time and destination.** Take the duration of your trip into consideration so that you won't have to carry a heavy bag over an extended period. Additionally, remember to check the weather forecast as well as the culture of your destination beforehand so you'll be fully prepared for your trip.

- **Prioritize the intention of the trip.** If, for example, you are heading out to take pictures, make sure to have all your camera gear and equipment. In another case, if you're going to the gym, prepare your gym clothes and gear, a change of clothes, and other things like a filled water bottle to keep hydrated as well as towels to dry off or take a shower at the gym.

- **Bring the essentials.** Don't forget to bring the crucial items like your ID/ passport, driving license, prescription glasses, or meds.

- **Use travel size.** If possible, try bringing the mini- or travel-size variant of the products you need. You won't be needing that entire 150ml of shampoo and conditioner for a 3-day trip. Keeping things travel-size will save valuable luggage space that you could either fill with other essentials or downsize your baggage significantly.

- **Ask yourself: "What items could be multi-purpose?"** For example, some sunscreens can also be used as foundation. Another example is choosing whether to bring several pocketbooks or just your Kindle.

When going out

- Maximizing the number of things you carry when going out is not necessarily better. The weight of a heavy bag or purse can be harmful to your shoulders or back and can lead to pain, stress, and irritation.

- You can start thinking about your bag basics, such as

  + Phone and charger

 + Cash and credit cards

  + Student or company ID

  + Other things like water bottles, iPad, or laptops, depending on your lifestyle

- Things that you shouldn't carry around all the time:

  + Flyers

  + Unused coupons

+ Bills and receipts

+ Extra jewelry, unnecessary make-up, and skincare products

+ Trash

-You should only bring essential items when going for a walk -

Traveling

The main difference between your luggage when traveling and everyday carry is the additional items. Due to the longer duration and farther distance, you should consider packing extra stuff in case of unexpected events. These "emergency items" could be extra underwear, phone and camera chargers, medicine, food, and the like.

As a traveler, I'm sure that "What-if's" and "Just-in-cases" would be popping up in your when whenever you start packing. It's always helpful to keep in mind the purpose of your trip. If it's a work trip, then an extra laptop charger and copies of important work-related documents may come in handy. On the other hand, if you're going on a fun holiday, you might, instead, bring extra camera gear or board games so you can have the best time with friends.

When packing, calmly evaluate each item before putting it on the list of things to bring. Specifically, you can try to compare different shirts or other items to see which one earns its space in the bag. Again, it may likely take some time and trial and error. However, this step will save you the mountains of stress when you end up lugging all that weight from the unnecessary things on your shoulders.

Another crucial element is getting the right bag. I'd advise primarily getting a smaller bag than what you might think necessary. When space is more limited than usual, you will think more carefully about what you will bring with you.

I also highly recommend choosing a bag that has various compartments, pockets, and straps. These features will let you pack more efficiently as well as more conveniently since you'd be able to pack similar items in one specific place. If time permits, you can also check the material, safety features, and comfort level of the bag to make sure your trip will be a great experience.

Moreover, you could think back on your past traveling experiences to figure out which items you rarely use and the items you always forget to bring.

Lastly, make sure you've thoroughly cleaned and taken out of the bag, all the items you brought from your last trip.

- You need to consider a few factors to pack sensibly -

Next time you travel, try bringing nothing but the items on the checklist and see what happens:

- Your passport / ID
- Money:
    - Credit cards
    - Cash
- Tools:
    - Headphones
    - Phone and charger
    - Laptop and charger
- Toiletries:
    - Toothbrush and toothpaste
    - Tissue paper
    - Soap
    - Lotion
    - Deodorant
    - 1-2 skincare products
- Clothes:
    - Pants (+1 extra), a skirt, and shorts
    - Two pieces of each top: shirts, jackets, sweaters,
    - Three pairs of underwear (+1 extra) and socks

CHAPTER III: SIMPLIFY DIGITAL WORLD

1. Why digital minimalism?

Nowadays, the space you have is not just confined to physical ones like your house or office. It also includes your digital space. The time you spend interacting with your digital space may even be longer than the time you spend with your family and friends. Try to think of your digital space as the space created by the Internet, including social media, remote work, or phone applications.

Here are some crucial elements to a minimalist digital lifestyle:

- **Just enough:** You will still use and enjoy the fantastic tools that have forever transformed our lives like the Internet, our computers, and our phones. However, it should be you who's in control, not them. You must only use them as needed to create meaning and value. When you take back control, you won't easily drown in the latest technology.

- **Optimize your toolbox:** It's fascinating how the ever-improving tools that are meant to enhance productivity can actually hinder us when we become too preoccupied with finding the perfect one. Consequently, we end up neglecting the actual work. Sometimes, the answer is not to add more, but to find a creative solution.

- **Say goodbye to FOMO:** FOMO, or fear of missing out, is the anxiety and fear you may experience when you think about an upcoming exciting event that you cannot attend. It is often made worse by all the fun social media posts that you might see on from that event. A good example is when you choose to stay at home on the weekend to recharge. However, you get upset when you see your friends partying in the city. Or, It may have been during a time when you really needed to focus on a project that you cared about. Still, you find yourself heartbroken after seeing your friend's Instagram post about her exciting trip. We have all been there. Everyone knows that living with anxiety is not fun. However, it does not have to be a part of your life anymore.

Your digital space is an extended version of your daily life. With all the time and energy we spend on our phones and computers, digital minimalism becomes equally important as any of your daily minimalism practices. Reducing the time you spend looking at screens will free up so much time and energy that you can use to be more productive.

- Our digital spaces have become an integral part of life -

2. Non-digital activities

The most obvious and possibly the hardest way to start your minimalist digital lifestyle is to reduce the activities wherein you use technology. Instead of spending your weekends watching Netflix, why don't you go out and plan a picnic with your closest friends? Rather than take notes on your laptop, use a notebook and a favorite pen. You can do this even with the simplest of activities. For example, you can use an analog clock instead of your phone, so you won't be tempted to spend the first hour of your day surfing the net.

Here are some rules you can apply to minimize your digital activities:

- **Find time for solitude.** Technology is invented to keep us connected to other parts of the world. However, some time alone could be helpful for you to recharge, especially if you are an introvert. How about leaving your phone behind and take a stroll in a park? Without touching your phone, you will feel less pressured to keep up with the exciting events around.

- **Limit phone application use.** Social media has slowly but surely become a key part of our life. Everyone taps that "Like" and "Share" button without thinking. Websites now can take that information and deliberately send addictive content into our phones or our computers to keep us hooked. Start being aware of that problem right now and limit your interaction with phone applications.

- **Find your hobbies and leisure activities.** Find your way back to the time before the smartphone and the addiction after that. What kept people occupied? They had hobbies and other leisure activities that they enjoyed. For you, it could be swimming, painting, reading, or building; try not to include shopping as a hobby, though.

I know that making the switch to a minimalist digital life is not easy. Getting rid of the unnecessary technological tools in your life so suddenly, especially in our fast-paced society can take some time. To give you a boost, I've given you the following tips so that you could keep both your digital space and clarity of mind at the same time.

3. Decluttering your email inbox

Have you ever woken up, checked your email, and felt overwhelmed by the number of unread messages in your inbox? They are probably mostly promotional and unimportant emails. However, seeing them piling up to three or four-digits can have the power to make you feel bad. So, what can we do about it?

There is a concept called Inbox Zero, developed by productivity expert Merlin Mann. It means that whenever you open your Gmail or other email services, except for newly arrived emails, the number of old emails in your inbox must always be zero.

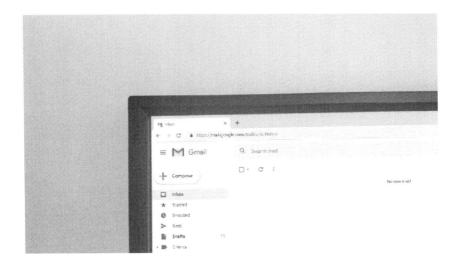

-Your email inbox does not have to be always full -

The effect of this change is that you will have a clearer and less stressed mind upon opening your email.

To achieve Inbox Zero for Gmail, follow this instruction guide:

Step 1: Sidebar and Categories

You could start by looking at your inbox's Sidebar to see the current state of your Gmail display.

Click on Setting > Labels. Here, you could decide on the primary features you want to have on your Email display. By default, your Gmail will have Inbox, Starred, Snoozed, Sent, and Drafts on the left side and categories like Primary, Social, Promotions, and Updates.

Depending on your habits and what this email is for, you can customize them however you want and need. My suggestion is to keep the left sidebar the same, hide the Snoozed feature, and keep Categories display with only two types: Primary and Updates.

Step 2: Start organizing your inbox

Now, we will officially start cleaning up your inbox! Look at the left sidebar and hit More.

Afterward, scroll down and click "Create new label" which will then open a window. If you can't find the "Create new label" option, it's at the very bottom of the sidebar, so just keep scrolling until you see it. The window or box that appears will let you create a new label/folder as well as give you the option to nest folders within other folders.

You can create different folders to categorize your emails. My suggestion is to create three folders, namely 1_PERSONAL, 2_WORK, and 3_ARCHIVES. The number and uppercase characters will make it easy for your eyes to track information. Also, don't forget to attach a different color to each label. Within each main folder, you can create nested folders with more specific labels. For example, folder 2_WORK might contain the folders 1_Office work, 2_Freelancer, 3_Part-time job, and so on. The label colors of the nested folders should be the same as its parent folder. This method gives you a lot of flexibility when organizing whatever your lifestyle or email needs may be. A tip, though, is not to have too many sub-labels. You should try to decide the direction that most of the emails will be pointing. There is always the option of naming a sub-label as Others.

Now, you could look into your enormous inbox and sort emails into the newly made labels while you move the unimportant emails to the Trash.

In the end, you will see your inbox empty and have all the important emails sorted into categories that are accessible and easy to find.

Step 3: Maintain the system

After you finish sorting the emails that are already in your inbox, you should slow down and enjoy the feeling of victory and satisfaction. Soon, however, new emails will come and sweep your inbox again. Don't worry. I've included helpful tips to maintain this system as well as your clear mind and heart:

- **"Starred" feature:** Click on the star in the email notification to mark an email when you don't have the time to file it into your categorized folders.
- **Extensive archive:** When you open an email, you'll see the Archive button right next to the Back button above the contents of the email. after archiving an email, you can still find it but it won't be in any of your folders.

- **Search bar:** Quickly find any email you want, even the ones that have not yet been permanently deleted in the Trash folder.

- **Unsubscribe from unnecessary newsletters, memberships, and promos:** Doing so is the fastest way to reduce the number of emails in your inbox.

- **Declutter daily:** Keeping your inbox tidy should follow the same principle for decluttering your house – you should do it everyday. If you spend just a little bit of time, as short as five to ten minutes, you will find this system very easy to maintain.

If possible, you should respond to new messages in two minutes or less.

4. Organize folders

Whatever job you have or how much technology you use, there will always be data that needs storing. I will introduce a simple way to organize your file structures so you could find any information in an instant.

-When was the last time you felt hopeless because you couldn't find an important file? -

Just as you would your actual desktop where your computer sits, we can apply the same rule with your inbox and create a blank desktop. If a completely blank screen is not possible on your phone, try to limit the number of items on it from five to seven things. You will feel completely different whenever you see your home screen.

If you have less than 15 GB data, I would advise you to store your files on Google Drive and categorize them into folders such as 1_PERSONAL, 2_JOBS, 3_ARCHIVE, and so on. Don't forget to pick different colors for each folder, ideally the same colors you used for Gmail. Also, you should get the Get Backup and Sync application installed. With this application, your data will automatically update from both your Google Drive and computer.

5. Goodbye phone addiction

Have you ever felt that your phone has become so smart that it has taken over your time, energy, and, ultimately, your life? Whatever kind or whichever brand of smartphone you have, the following practices will help you regain control.

- **No social media and messaging applications or shortcuts.** You'll be less tempted to reach for your phone out of boredom and end up wasting hours randomly scrolling newsfeeds or unnecessary chats with friends. You'll be much more conscious of your time if you would need to open Safari or Google Chrome, type in "Twitter," and log in to your account. Also, avoid keeping shortcuts of the social media apps where they're easy to find.

- Use the **"Do not disturb"** mode when you need to go to bed or when you have important and urgent tasks.

- How much time do you spend on your phone daily? -

- **Greyscale feature.** This mode will washout your phone's color into black and white. Thus, it will be much less interesting to look at or use, and the chances of it distracting you will be much lower. Here's how you can enable this mode:

    o On Android devices: Go to Settings > About phone > Software information and tap on the Build number until you see a message saying, "you are now a developer." When seeing a message announcing that you are a developer now, you have activated your Developer options. Then you could go to Settings > Advanced settings > Developer options > Hardware Accelerated Rendering > Simulate color space > Monochromacy.

o On iOS devices: Go to Settings > General > Accessibility and find Display Accommodations. Afterward, switch on Color Filters and choose Grayscale. To make it a shortcut, go to Settings > General > Accessibility. After that, select Accessibility Shortcut and Color Filters. This shortcut will be a double-edged sword, though since it'll make turning off the feature as easy as turning it on.

- **Sort apps.** Categorize your phone applications into groups of similar features like Camera, Productivity, Entertainment, etc. It will help you avoid feeling stressed and lost whenever you're looking at your phone screen and seeing the disorganized mess.

- **Track your phone usage.** It may shock you to know how much time you actually spend looking at your phone. If you use it for 5-6 hours a day, it'll mean a quarter of your life. With an application like Screen time on iOS or Digital Wellbeing on Android, you'll even see the specific applications that eat up most of your time. You might be justifying that you're using your phone for work when 80% of your screen time is actually used for Instagram and Snapchat. These applications will help you realize just how much time you're using.

6. Social media

It is undeniable that social media has become so beneficial for us. It strengthens our connection with our loved ones and can spread meaningful messages all over the world. On the other hand, it can also destroy many beautiful things like family time, your productivity, and possibly your self-confidence. Let me give you some advice to minimize the damage that social media can bring:

- **Prioritize:** What are 5,000 Facebook friends when the number of your real-life friends is zero? To have more time and energy to focus on the relationships that really matter, you may want to limit the number of accounts you're following on any platform to 200 or less. You might have to make some tough decisions unfriending or unfollowing people, but it'll be worth it when your inbox and newsfeed filled only with meaningful messages.

- **Limit social media use:** You can easily find applications for your phone and computer that will help you curb your social media usage. For example, you could use Screen time, Moments, Offtime for your phone. On your computer, you could use Chrome extensions like Block Site or applications like Focusme and Freedom.

- **Join the Social Media Detox movement:** Decide on a specific period when you'll eliminate social media out of your life. It could be as long as a month, or as short as a week or even day. The most important thing is that, at the end of this experiment, you will realize that your life is still excellent without social media, or even better. You might rediscover your old habits, reconnect with your real friends, and have quality time with yourself. In case of emergencies, you could leave an email address on your social media so that people know how to get in touch with you.

7. Daily practices

It might be easy to advise you to quit social media or even dispose of your phone altogether, but we all know that it will be a long and hard journey to eliminate the influence of social media on our lives. However, what we can all do now is keep reminding ourselves of the possible consequences of letting our technology decide our future. To help you on this attempt, here are some notes:

- **Do not check your social media or messages until noon.** For many people, mornings are when your mind is most relaxed and ready for creative activities. Are you going to let this time go to waste on social media and continually checking your Gmail every 10 minutes? You won't be able to start your day correctly with one hour of scrolling through social media. In exceptional cases, your work may not allow you to do this. Otherwise, you should try to limit Internet usage in the morning as much as possible

- **Do not use your phone in bed.** It's undeniable that smartphones are fascinating. We can get so hooked that we don't notice the time while away. This situation gets worse when you are in bed and ready to relax. You will likely forget the time and lose yourself in your phone. You should either put the phone on Airplane mode or place as far away from your bed as possible.

- **Do not take your phone to the bathroom.** It is not only very unhygienic but also robs you of your break time.

- **Turn off notifications, badges, and sounds and use an adblocker.** You will not be able to focus on your work when a notification pops up or rings every 2 seconds.

- Install a Habit tracking app so that you could see how you are spending your day and manage it better.

- Use **bookmarks** and **password management** on your web engine to reduce unnecessary wastes of time.

- **Schedule** the time you use social media and other tools so that you will not get lost in them. An alarm could be useful in this situation

- **Read books instead of news.** Sometimes, it could be so tempting to check the news like you would your messages. With all the headlines and clickbait, you may lose your confidence in the fight for your attention.

- **Practice mindful eating.** Try to savor the tastes, the scents, and the visuals of the food, instead of watching the latest Netflix release.

- **Set daily deadlines** so that you are more deliberate with your time while you're using your devices.

Chapter IV: Useful tips

1. Find a home for your old friends

After every decluttering session, most people may feel bitter or upset after bidding farewell to their belongings. It doesn't have to be that way. Quite the contrary, you will feel happier than ever before because you will have the chance to bring happiness to other people's lives. Remember the Giveaway and Trash bundle that we mentioned above. Now, I will give you a few excellent suggestions about what to do with them.

Donate

Sometimes, it's hard to admit that you have more than the necessities while there are people out there struggling to make ends meet. This practice is the ideal opportunity to take things into perspective that some people may not be born with the same privileges as you and would appreciate your help. That lamp you have always kept in your storage room since you bought it can make such a difference for a family with several children working daily to power enough light to study at night.

You could find the receiver yourself. The ones in need may be closer than you think. They could be your neighbors, your co-workers, or your relatives. Additionally, you could donate to a church, social organizations, or visit websites like Pickupplease.org, Charitynavigator.org, and Good360.org.

If you have any special items or artifacts, you could donate them to the local museum or exhibition.

-Donating is an excellent way to let go of your belongings -

Sell

Even if you don't need the money, this practice may add an unexpected significant sum of cash into your bank account. You could perhaps get back the money that you spent on compulsive shopping.

As the Internet continues to evolve, it has become so easy to buy and sell online. You could go to eBay, Facebook groups, Letgo, Offerup, and so on to earn some cash from selling your old furniture. If your buyers are near your area, you could pack and ship the item yourself. Some people find this process especially therapeutic, saying goodbye to their old possessions.

Ultimately, you are happy with some extra spending money, and the buyer is satisfied with a decent once-loved item. Moreover, this practice also contributes to saving the resources required for manufacturing new products.

Swap parties

If you have people in your community who pursue the same meaningful and simple life just like you, it will be much less likely that you will give up halfway. That sense of community can be powerful. Let me introduce you to the swap party.

A swap party is a gathering where people get together and swap or trade items. You could take the initiative and organize everything yourself, or you could invite some friends to co-host the party with you.

You could plan it any way you want. It could be a private event where only your friends and acquaintances will be present, or it could be a public event where you could meet your friends' friends. The only rule of thumb here is that you should make decisions based on your resources such as time, money, and your preferences.

My advice is to throw a small test party and learn from it. So, if you want to host a bigger one, you'll be better equipped, and the risks will be lower. You can also merge it with a BBQ party, a picnic, or a warm reunion. No matter what form and shape it takes, as long as you do not forget the primary mission (to SWAP), it will be beautiful.

Here are some important steps to organize a Swap party:

Step 1: Decide on the guest list

When you finalize on your Swap party's attendees, it will be much easier to make other decisions like the venue, the schedule, itinerary, and how it's to be organized.

If you are unsure about who would be interested in joining your party, you could create a Google Form or a post on your social media and observe other people's reactions. Thus, you'll have a better idea about the possible size of the party and who you would like to invite.

When you're finalizing the guest list, remember to put it on an Excel sheet that will help you to check-in on people.

- *A Swap party is a chance to make connections -*

Step 2: Create some party rules

When it begins, the party could get chaotic fast. To minimize that risk, you should set some ground rules to guarantee that everyone will have a good time. Some simple rules could include:

- **What to bring and what not to bring:** You should make it clear that everyone has to bring products that are in good condition. If you want to be more specific, you could establish a theme for the party. For example, attendees will only swap clothes or books or kitchenware. It could bring a fantastic twist to the event.
- Set the **maximum or the minimum** number of items.
- **Timeline:** will the party go on for the entire day, or will people trade for a specific period and the lead to the party later?
- **Remind people** to clean up after themselves and be aware of litter.
- Remember to **announce the rules** to everyone before the party and remind them of it on the day.

Step 3: Get the detailed tasks done

Because this is an event with potentially numerous participants, the responsibility of organizing could be burdensome. Like I have suggested above, you could invite other people to share the load. Most importantly, you could make a checklist to control the workflow. The list should at least include:

- **Finding a space:** Look for a suitable space that can accommodate your party's size and its planned activities. It could be your house, a friend's house, the park, or even a small church. Ideally, it should be free of rent.
- **Find supplies** for the party, such as name cards, markers, tables, chairs, etc.
- **Prepare food and drink:** Simple snacks and water should be adequate, but other options will be up to you. You could even sell food if you want and profit from it.

Step 4: Send your invitations and wish for the best

Don't forget to send the invite and check for the guests' confirmation. After all,we have done, we are not going to stop at this step, right?

Step 5: Enjoy the party

There are many ways to organize a party. The easiest way is to sort items and put them on separate tables but specific areas, such as accessories, clothes, baking tools, and so on. The last step is to place a big sign at each area. Thus, you will not have to spend too much energy explaining, organizing, and guiding.

If this is the first party you host, you may make some mistakes; some guests may misbehave, some things may not go according to your plans. No matter what happens, be proud that you created something amazing from nothing.

Step 6: Build a connection with the community

After the party, you should spend some time to thank people for coming and send emails or messages so you can get feedback from your participants. If the party goes well and everybody has a good time, you could even make a Facebook group so that people could keep in touch with each other and spread the word about minimalism.

Recycling and upcycling

The practice of recycling and upcycling gives the items in your Trash pile another chance. You could use this method to breathe new life into things you only intend to throw away. The only limit here is your imagination.

You can quickly find ideas or suggestions online with websites like Pinterest and Instagram.

Simple upcycling ideas are:

- Using your old jars to create decorative lights
- Turning an old tea container into a plant pot.
- Recycle old car tires into a garden decoration

A small warning: Being creative with upcycling can be incredibly fun and fulfilling. However, avoid buying new unnecessary stuff because of upcycling.

Compost

Here is an essential guide for you to start composting at home. This practice will reduce your trash waste and lead towards a greener lifestyle.

- Necessary **composting tools**
- **Kitchen container with lid:** Its job is to contain the compostable items in the kitchen, ready for the next stage. You should only buy a new one if you have absolutely no other container at home with which you could replace it. Remember to keep it where the smell will not be a problem.
- **A compost bin outdoors.** It could be in your garden or your balcony or rooftop. It should be significantly bigger than the compost container in your kitchen and kept close enough to your house so it won't be difficult to reach.

- Some **extra tools** are a scrap collector and a scrap sack. They are not compulsory, but depending on the situation of your house and habits; they may make your life easier.

How to do it?

Step 1: Kitchen preparation

Several things in your kitchen are potential compost, such as vegetable scraps, fruit peels, eggshells, shredded paper bags, coffee grounds, and the like. You could put all of them in your kitchen compost container.

Step 2: Real compost

When you notice that your kitchen's compost container is almost full or gets too smelly, it's the right time to empty it into the outdoor container. Then, all you have to do is wait for composting to do its magic.

-Compost could bring so much value and nutrition into your garden-

Step 3: Enjoy the results

You can use your finished compost in numerous ways. One of them is as a soil topper or a soil mix to be used for flower and vegetable beds. It can also help revitalize indoor plants. Overall, compost helps improve the structure and overall health of your soil significantly.

2. Take it easy

One of the tips to make any habit stick is to make it ridiculously easy. You do not have to declutter your whole house no matter how excited you are to make changes. If you feel too burdened and lazy because of the size of the task at hand, break it into tiny parts and do it for 5 minutes daily. After that, you will have the drive to do it for longer periods. If you can't do all the work in one day, break it down into different parts and do it on the weekends or whenever you have free time. If you become tired in the middle of it, you could take a break, check your phone, read a book, and then come back.

If you are a forgetful person or need the motivation to get the work done, you could try to make a checklist of all the necessary tasks as well as a timeline with deadlines.

For example, your checklist could look like this

- Weekend 1: Declutter and organize my wardrobe
- Weekend 2: Plan to give away clothes and start checking my bedroom
- Weekend 3: Clean my bedroom and start decluttering the walls, the bookshelf, and the bed, etc.

The satisfying feeling of crossing a line, ticking a box after finishing a task could give you the encouragement you need on the road to becoming a minimalist.

3. Don't compare your progress to others

No matter how many times I tell you that changing a lifestyle is not a competition, you may still feel defeated and upset when you come across an Instagram post from somebody who seems to be happier with even fewer belongings. When negative feelings like that come up, you should hold your breath and calm down. Tell yourself that you are making an effort, and you have worked hard!

Instead of sitting in one place comparing yourself to others, take before and after pictures, and compare your progress. I am sure you will see a clear difference and feel your life has completely transformed.

4. Don't stop

Like any other habit, it's easy for us to get off track when life gets in the way. We all purchase stuff compulsively without planning when going into stores. Therefore, you will have to declutter several times in your life. To do that effectively, you could set a monthly review or twice annually, depending on your preference and needs.

5. Have fun!

The final goal of all this work is to bring more happiness into your life, so don't put yourself under too much pressure and try to do it correctly on the first try. You will gain experience and do it with more confidence with time and practice.

Final words

As I have told you many times in this book, to seek a meaningful life by decluttering (both in the physical world and digital space) is not a task that you can finish in one or two days. It is a process; a lifestyle that you need to maintain. You will find challenges along the way, but it will be worth it. As change takes time to make a real impact on your life, you should be kind and patient with yourself along your journey. What's important is that compare yourself to who you were yesterday, not to somebody else.

More importantly, it is about your mindset on letting go of things that do not matter to make space for the truly important things into your life with appreciation and love. You will have a calmer and less agitated mind. Hopefully, you could also make better decisions with a clearer state of mind. You will have more time and energy to intentionally put the focus on the factors that bring joy in your life. Freedom is not far off; it is right there in your hand.

I sincerely wish you luck in this journey to a better life and to become a better person!

Thank you for reading this book!

-- By Chloe White --

W-8   £1.99 NC

Printed in Great Britain
by Amazon